CARRIE UNDERWOOD

American Dream

by Riley Brooks

SCHOLASTIC INC.

Photographs copyright © 2013:

AP Images: 4 (Mark Humphrey); 20 (Diane Bondareff/PictureGroup)

Getty Images: Cover (Jon Kopaloff/FilmMagic); cover inset (Erika Goldring);
1 (Kevin Winter/WireImage); 2 (Frederick Breedon/FilmMagic); 3 (Duffy-Marie Arnoult/WireImage);
5 & 6 (Ray Mickshaw/WireImage); 9 (Kevin Winter); 10 (Richard Corkery/NY Daily News Archive);
13 (Larry Busacca/WireImage); 19 (Richard Foreman/CBS); 23 (Rick Diamond), 24 (Neilson Barnard)

Newscom/Will Binns, PacificCoastNews: 16

© 2013 by Scholastic
ISBN 978-0-545-62189-2

Published by Scholastic Inc.
SCHOLASTIC and associated logos are trademarks and/or registered trademarks of Scholastic Inc.

12 11 10 9 8 7 6 5 4 3 2 1   13 14 15 16 17 18/0

Printed in the U.S.A.   40
First printing, September 2013

TABLE OF CONTENTS

INTRODUCTION

With four bestselling albums under her belt in just eight years, there's no denying that Carrie Underwood is the reigning queen of country music. She's one of the biggest names in entertainment, having won multiple awards and toured all over the world, but Carrie's road to super-stardom wasn't as easy as you might think. After a failed record deal sidelined her when she was a teenager, Carrie almost gave up on her dream to be a professional singer. She was pursuing a career as a news anchor when she got her second chance, and, that time, Carrie fought with everything she had and was able to achieve more than she ever thought possible. Carrie is proof that if you keep working, there's no dream you can't make come true!

Chapter 1

ON HER WAY

Before she became a country music megastar, Carrie grew up as just a regular girl in the small town of Checotah, Oklahoma. She was born on March 10, 1983, to parents Stephen and Carole Underwood. Stephen worked at a paper mill and Carole taught elementary school. Carrie realized she had musical talent when she started singing in her church choir. When Carrie was only thirteen years old, she traveled to Nashville and auditioned for Capitol Records. They offered her a record deal, but canceled it when management inside of the company changed. Carrie was devastated that it didn't work out, but she didn't let it stop her from singing. She sang at church and her high school, where she was also a cheerleader, basketball and softball player, and an honor student.

After high school, Carrie decided to focus on journalism instead of music, and she went to Northeastern State University in Oklahoma to get her college degree in journalism. Carrie loved college and was excited to pursue a career after school, but a little part of her held out hope that singing might still be a part of her future. In early 2005, Carrie got her chance at a big break when she auditioned for the TV singing competition show *American Idol*.

After working her way through several grueling rounds of auditions, Carrie made it onto the show and was an early favorite to win. The judges loved her strong, big voice, and fans adored her energetic performances — she got top scores almost every single week. Scores of fans calling themselves "Carrie's Care Bears" called in to vote for Carrie each week, and no one was surprised when she made it to the finals. After singing the country hit "Bless the Broken Road" alongside Rascal Flatts, Carrie won the show! It was the most amazing moment of her life, as Carrie explained to Collider.com. "*American Idol* is

THE biggest television show of my generation," she said. "To be a part of the show and the brand, and a part of everything that has come since then, there are a few people that can say that, and I'm very honored to be one of those people." As the winner, Carrie got a recording contract with a major music label. Nine years after her first chance, Carrie was finally heading to Nashville to record her debut album!

Chapter 2

ALL-AMERICAN ALBUMS

Now that her dream had finally come true, Carrie couldn't wait to get started on her singing career. But she wanted to do it her way. All of the previous *American Idol* winners had focused on pop and rock music, but Carrie was only interested in country music. Luckily, her label was on board. They paired her up with great country songwriters and producers to record *Some Hearts*, which released in November 2005. Fans went wild for Carrie's music and it became the bestselling country album in America for all of 2006 and 2007. It was eventually certified platinum seven times, meaning it sold more than seven million copies — Carrie Underwood was officially a country star! She spent the next two years touring and promoting her debut album before finally finding some time to head into the recording studio again.

In October 2007, Carrie's second album, *Carnival Ride*, hit store shelves. Her second time around, Carrie was even more involved in the recording process than she had been the first time. She held a special retreat in

Nashville with veteran songwriters to work on new songs and select the choices for her album. The result were standout singles like "All-American Girl," "So Small," "Last Name," and "Just a Dream" that really cemented Carrie's title as country music's sweetheart. The album ended up going triple platinum and Carrie spent the next two years touring and doing promotions.

In November 2009, *Play On*, Carrie's third album, debuted at the top of the charts. Singles like "Mama's Song," "Undo It," and "Temporary Home" were played nonstop on the radio. The same year, she recorded a duet with Brad Paisley called "Remind Me" that hit number one on the country charts.

Carrie helped write most of the songs on her fourth album, *Blown Away*, which debuted at number one on the country and all-genre

charts in May 2012. Singles such as "Good Girl," "Blown Away," and "Two Black Cadillacs" all still feature Carrie's signature big sound and incredible vocal range. As Carrie explained on CarrieUnderwoodOfficial.com, "I love this album from start to finish and love every song on it. There's not one single song that's like another song I've ever done. I think it's my best album. I really do think there's something for everyone." She launched her Blown Away tour, her biggest ever, to support the album and hit the road with Hunter Hayes as her opening act in June 2012.

Hunter is a rising star in the country world and Carrie has really enjoyed working with him, as she explained in an interview with HeadlineCountry.net. "He's so talented and such a nice guy. He works incredibly hard. He's already doing so well and for him, still, there's no where to go but up." The two of them made the perfect pair for such an epic tour! In fact, the tour was so huge that in June 2013 it had its own exhibition at the Country Music Hall of Fame!

Carrie's albums have been big hits with her fans, but they've also earned her the respect of everyone in the music industry. She's won six Grammy Awards, sixteen Billboard Music Awards, ten Academy of Country Music Awards, seven American Music Awards, six People's Choice Awards, five Country Music Association Awards, nine CMT Awards, nine American Country Music Awards, seven Broadcast Music, Inc. Awards, and numerous others. She's sold over fifteen million albums and twenty-seven million singles. It's been a crazy ride for Carrie, but she's loved every single minute of it!

Chapter 3

BEYOND THE MUSIC

C arrie may be most well-known for her powerhouse voice, but she's expanded her career far beyond her bestselling albums. Carrie has been the face of big brands like Olay beauty products and vitaminwater, but she spends most of her time on the road, touring for her fans. She was ranked as the top-selling female country music touring artist for her Carnival Ride tour in 2008 and her Play On tour in 2010. Carrie has performed all around the world, and most of her concerts sell out. She's one hot ticket!

Carrie has also had the opportunity to perform with some of the biggest names in music. She sang with Steven Tyler from the rock band Aerosmith on CMT's "Crossroads," performed Tony Bennett's classic "It Had to Be You" with him at the 2012 Grammy Awards, and has performed alongside Celine Dion, Usher, Smokey Robinson, and Jennifer Hudson. Carrie has hosted the CMA Awards five different times with cohost Brad Paisley, who is also a good friend of Carrie's. In 2008, Randy Travis and Garth Brooks inducted Carrie into the Grand Ole Opry, one of the most exclusive clubs in country music, and she's performed there more than thirty-seven times.

Acting is something that Carrie is still pretty new to, but she's loved getting the chance to try it. She's recorded several songs for movie soundtracks such as *The Chronicles of Narnia: The Dawn Treader* and *Enchanted*, but her first time appearing onscreen in a scripted role was in 2010 when Carrie guest-starred on the hit show *How I Met Your Mother*. Carrie was delightfully funny. With that success under her belt, Carrie made her film debut in 2011's *Soul Surfer*, which was based on a true story. "When I read the script, I definitely wanted to be involved. It's such an inspirational story," Carrie explained to Collider.com. In the film, surfer Bethany Hamilton loses her arm to a shark attack and then must learn to surf all over again. Carrie played Sarah Hill,

Bethany's youth group leader. For her next big role, Carrie will play the role of Maria von Trapp in a remake of *The Sound of Music*, a three-hour special that will debut on NBC in late 2013. Carrie loves acting and will most likely continue to take on roles in the future, but music will always be her biggest priority.

Chapter 4

BEHIND THE SCENES

C arrie spends most of her time working, but she does manage to take a little time off whenever she can. She lives near Nashville, Tennessee, with her husband, Mike Fisher, a professional hockey player for the Nashville Predators, and her two dogs.

Carrie loves to support her husband, and can often be found at Predators' games cheering him on. She and Mike love watching sports and both work out often — they're a very active couple!

Animals are one of Carrie's biggest passions. She's a vegetarian and says she is 95% vegan as well. Carrie adopted both of her dogs from animal shelters and has always encouraged her fans to do the same. She has done several public service announcements in support of animal safety and adoption. Carrie has also worked with the dog food company Pedigree on adoption drives and to raise money for animal shelters.

Of course, animal charities aren't the only ones Carrie works with. She has also established a special charity in her hometown called the Checotah Animal,

Town, and School Foundation, which helps community members who are most in need. She plays in Nashville's City of Hope Celebrity Softball tournament every year to raise money for research of life-threatening diseases. In addition, St. Jude's Children's Research Hospital, Save the Children, the United Service Organization, Clothes Off Our Back, Habitat for Humanity, the American Red Cross, and Stand Up to Cancer have all received help from Carrie over the years. Carrie and her husband even made a special video urging kids to stop bullying. Giving back is very important to this country star—Carrie might have a big voice, but she has an even bigger heart!

So what does the future hold for a superstar like Carrie? Plenty more music, that's for sure! Carrie plans to put out a new album

INTRODUCTION

It's not often that a new country star tops the charts with his very first album, but that's exactly what twenty-two-year-old, blue-eyed country cutie Hunter Hayes did! He burst onto the country music scene in 2011 with an award-winning album that really stood out. Not only did Hunter write or cowrite every song on the album, but he also played every single instrument on every single song—now that's some serious talent! He's been busy ever since touring, performing, writing new songs, and racking up awards. Country music loves Hunter, and, luckily for all of Hunter's new fans, it looks like he's here to stay!

STAR ON THE RISE

Hunter Hayes was born to be a star on September 9, 1991, in Breaux Bridge, Louisiana. He began playing the accordion when he was only two years old. By the time he was four, Hunter had formed a band and was performing all over Louisiana. He even appeared on TV a few times, and he got to play his accordion and sing "Jambalaya (On the Bayou)" — a classic Cajun song— alongside country music legend Hank Williams Jr. His parents should have known then that Hunter was destined for country-music superstardom!

When Hunter was six, he was selected by actor Robert Duvall to play a small role in the film *The Apostle*. Robert even came to Hunter's birthday party and gave him his first guitar as a gift. That guitar sparked Hunter's interest in songwriting. "At school, I was a quiet kid," Hunter explains on his website, HunterHayes.com. "I was really shy. My safe zone was music. In writing music, I had my friend, the one thing that would never let me down. Writing songs was like me keeping a journal. I really took it seriously when I realized how powerful of a tool it was and how much I needed it."

By the time Hunter was a teenager, he knew without a doubt that he wanted to be a country music star. He recorded several albums himself before deciding he wanted to try to get a real record deal. He was so serious about it that he spent more time performing at gigs

than he did at school dances or parties. "I voluntarily skipped out on a lot," Hunter explained on HunterHayes.com. "I was working on song demos. That was the one thing that was going really well. I was going to give every minute to it that I possibly could."

Luckily, Hunter's parents were very supportive of their son's dreams, and so the whole family moved to Nashville, Tennessee, when Hunter was only sixteen. He finished high school that same year through an online school program, and then set out to get a record deal. "I made a promise to myself that as soon as I finished

that course, I was going to write at least a song a week," Hunter explained on HunterHayes.com. "In fact, that first week, I wrote a song every day." Hunter's dedication paid off—he recorded an EP called *Songs About Nothing*, featuring his original songs. He played every single instrument on the EP. Atlantic Records loved it and signed Hunter to a record deal when he was nineteen years old.

ONE-MAN BAND

f Hunter was nervous to walk into a studio and record his first full album, he didn't let it show. He worked with producer Dann Huff to narrow down sixty songs he'd written to the twelve that ended up on his self-titled debut album. Then Hunter and Dann spent the next several months in the studio, where Hunter sang and played every instrument for every song. It was the first time anyone in the country music industry had attempted anything like it, since most artists record with a backup band of professional musicians.

But Hunter's dedication and hard work really paid off! "Storm Warning," the first single from his album, *Hunter Hayes*, debuted on May 16, 2011, and instantly became a radio hit. Taylor Swift loved the song so much that she invited Hunter to open for her on her Speak Now world tour that summer. His full album went on sale on October 11, 2011, and Hunter spent the rest of the year touring to promote the album on his Most Wanted tour. Then in January 2012, Hunter went on tour with Rascal Flatts for several months. The guys of Rascal Flatts were already big Hunter fans since they had recorded his song "Play" in 2010. Going on tour with established country stars was really helpful for Hunter, and he learned a lot. Of his time touring with Taylor Swift, he told the *Baltimore Sun*, "I'm glad I made the effort to watch her [Taylor Swift's] show every night... I made notes; I was studying every night. I'm

a huge fan of hers. She takes a room of fifteen thousand people and you feel like you got to shake her hand, give her a hug. You feel like you know her after she leaves."

In March 2012, Hunter's second official single, "Wanted," was released. It quickly shot to number one on the country charts, was certified gold within a few months, and had gone platinum by August 2012. In fact, "Wanted" was so successful that it helped Hunter break a record. He became the youngest male solo act to top the Hot Country Songs charts since 1973. His next single, "Somebody's Heartbreak," reached number nine on the charts and is a big fan favorite. Chances are his next few singles will be just as successful, and fans are already eager to hear them on the radio.

HUNTER OFF STAGE

When Hunter wasn't busy touring to promote his first studio album, he was recording music videos for his songs and working with other artists. In addition to writing for other country acts, Hunter wrote the song "Where We Left Off" for the 2012 war movie *Act of Valor*, and it was included on the film's soundtrack. Hunter also recorded the classic song "Almost Paradise" for the movie *Footloose* with actress and singer Victoria Justice, star of Nickelodeon's *Victorious*. Hunter loves working with other artists, and they love working with him!

In May 2012, Hunter became the newest face of C.F. Martin & Co., a well-respected company that designs high-end guitars. Hunter loves their custom work and was thrilled to be asked to work with the famous brand. "It is an absolute honor to be named an official Martin Ambassador and to be recognized by the Martin family," Hunter told *American Songwriter* magazine. And that wasn't the only honor Hunter received in 2012. Just a few days before Hunter's twenty-first birthday, he became the youngest person ever inducted into the Louisiana Music Hall of Fame!

Hunter is also the youngest male country artist ever to be simultaneously nominated for Grammy Awards for Best New Artist, Best Country Solo Performance, and Best Country Album. Though he didn't win, it was still a huge honor to be nominated three times for his very first album. Luckily, Hunter had more luck

at some of the other award shows. He won a Teen Choice Award for Male Country Artist; a Broadcast Music, Inc., songwriting award for "Storm Warning"; the Country Music Association Award for New Artist of the Year and Single of the Year: New Artist; and the American Country Award for Music Video of the Year: New Artist for "Wanted." Hunter was also nominated in four categories at the forty-eighth annual Academy of Country Music Awards.

MORE TO COME

So what's up next for this versatile entertainer and songwriter? Plenty! Hunter has played more than ninety sold-out shows opening for Carrie Underwood as part of her Blown Away tour. He loves performing with Carrie, as he explained to MTV News, "She's a sweetheart. She's awesome. Her show is really impressive and it's kind of cool 'cause I'm a production guy and I'm really into watching shows and she's a consistent vocalist. It's really something I love to watch and it's intimidating 'cause you

sort of stand there and you're like, 'How do you do that?' It's unbelievable." Touring with such a huge country star has definitely helped Hunter improve his own performances. He told JustJaredJr.com, "We go back, watch the show, and critique it. We had about a month to think about it and to figure out what to do better." Hunter couldn't ask for a better teacher than Carrie!

Of course, being on tour hasn't stopped Hunter from working on his next album. He's been writing plenty of new songs, both for himself and for other musicians. He also found time to record some of his performances and has released a mini-album called *Hunter Hayes Live* that includes "Wanted," "Storm Warning," "Somebody's Heartbreak," "More Than I Should," and "Love Makes Me." It really gives fans a feel for what it's like to hear him sing up close and in person.

Hunter has also been busy making television appearances and giving his fans a chance to meet him in person. He's given interviews and performed on some of the biggest shows on TV, including *The Late Show with David Letterman*; *Good Morning America*; *Late Night with Jimmy Fallon*; *The Talk*; *E! News*; and *The Ellen DeGeneres Show*.

And he's not done yet—Hunter's schedule for the next year is full of appearances, performances, and, of course, lots of song-writing. "My goal has always been to be an artist. I love where I am right now, in the back of a tour bus. . . . I write for myself," Hunter told the *Arizona Republic*. "I don't write because I have a record coming out. I write because I want to. I need to. . . . I want to do this for the rest of my life." Luckily for Hunter's fans, it sounds like Hunter will be putting out great music for a long time to come!

JUST THE FACTS

Name: Hunter Easton Hayes
Birthday: September 9, 1991
Hometown: Breaux Bridge, Louisiana
Current Town: Nashville, Tennessee
Parents: Lynette and Leo Hayes
Siblings: none
Pets: a dog named Charlie
Height: 5'6"
Hair: dirty blonde
Eyes: blue
Instruments: guitar, accordion, keyboard, piano, drums, bass guitar, mandolin, and 23 other instruments
Hobbies: songwriting, flying (he's training for his pilot's license!), listening to music
Favorite Food: Cajun food
Favorite Color: red
Favorite Place to Spend Time: the recording studio he built at his house
Favorite Artists: Stevie Wonder, Keith Urban, and U2
Can't Live Without: coffee, his Martin guitar